Tom Pickard was born in 1946 in Newcastle upon Tyne and educated in Blakelaw, where he gained a last at Cowgate Secondary Modern. He has cobbled together a career ever since, between periods as a welfare claimant, as a writer, labourer, bookdealer, curator, dyker, driver, performer, librettist, oral historian, and producer-director of film and radio documentaries. A lifelong counter-culture figure, in 1964, aged eighteen, Pickard co-founded Morden Tower, a live poetry venue in Newcastle, hosting poets such as Allen Ginsberg, Robert Creeley, and Basil Bunting. In 1973 he moved to London, where he occasionally worked as a market trader and writer/director of radio, film and television documentaries, including *We Make Ships* (1988) and *The Shadow and the Substance* (1994). Pickard has collaborated throughout his career with musicians, film-makers and poets. He is the recipient of a Gold Medal from the New York International Film and TV Festival, and the 2011 Bess Hokin Prize for poetry. His publications include *High on the Walls* (1968), *Guttersnipe* (1971), *fuckwind* (1999), *The Dark Months of May* (2004), *Ballad of Jamie Allan* (2007) and *More Pricks Than Prizes* (2010).

T0159812

Also by TOM PICKARD
from Carcanet Press

hoyoot: Collected Poems and Songs
2014

WINTER MIGRANTS

TOM PICKARD

CARCANET

for Gill

First published in Great Britain in 2016 by
Carcanet Press Limited
Alliance House, 30 Cross Street,
Manchester, M2 7AQ
www.carcanet.co.uk

A CIP catalogue record for this book is
available from the British Library,
ISBN 9781784102647

The publisher acknowledges financial
assistance from Arts Council England.

Supported using public funding by
**ARTS COUNCIL
ENGLAND**

VALENTYNE

only you bring such gifts,
(and presence):

a curlew caller,
(I'm here, I hear),

and stone-age axe,
(what reach you have)

a flint heart splint from rock
sparks flame to fire

I clasp it
as I write

Contents

≈

LARK & MERLIN

1

a wren,
perched on a hawthorn
low enough to skip
the scalping winds,

sang a scalpel song

sea frets drift
sheer along shorelines

in a café without customers,
listening to hail spray glass,
and wind and a waitress laugh,
I fell to fell thinking

a sullen light through vapour
thins a line of hills

the edge of everything is nothing
whipped by wind

watched on a webcam
bound to a bedpost
gag on my shaft

rose blush of roadkill rabbit
insides out on Tarmacadam

cumulus in a tarn
its fast shadow
flees far hills

a wave of sleek grass
skiffs mist

my hand thought of her
a photograph
waiting to happen

this come-to-kill wind
rips at the root

here she comes
and there she goes
rushes bow to rime

I should shut down
close off
stop

if I could

how quick the mist
how quick

2

my lover, the assassin,
is beautiful

she has come to kill me
and I concur

just now she sleeps
but when she wakes I'm dead

her eyelids flitter
as I prepare her potions,
her delicious poisons

as she flew past a lick
of her melodic nectar
stuck to my wing,
making flight, for an instant,
sticky

but nothing preening couldn't fix

she asked about my heart,
its evasive flight;
but can I trust her with its secrets?

and does the merlin, in fast pursuit of its prey,
tell the fleeing lark it is enamoured of its song?

or the singing lark turn tail
and fly into the falcon's talons?

my heart, the cartographer, charts
to the waterline,
is swept back as the tide turns
wiping the map blank, wave
after moon-drawn wave

walking home I stride these tracks
with her tread

3

it has gone on for days

strumming rushes
taking up tales,
taking them on
the fall of my foot, on tufts

a stroke of light along a law lain in under a long cloud

I accrete – lichen to limestone
sphagnum to peat

late shadows gather in the dark

words unwrite
as they are written
unspeak
as they are spoken

songs sprung
from heart and lung
to tongue

unsung

drunk winds
stumble over shuffling roofs
shake his sleep who dreams
a lost love
will not
let
go

recurring swirls
of old gold
blown light

you can't help
but be in it

as it opens
and falls back on itself
unfolds and unsays

I do not want to die
without writing the unwritten

pleasure of water

AN OLD SONG

She said she would not dwell
In the heather on the fell
Beneath the down upon my bed
And all the words she said.

I'd rather be an old stairwell
And feel the weary tread
Than be an unsprung mattress
On your old cold bed.

I saw the midnight waters rise
The colour of her eyes.

PROLOGUE

When my lover became my enemy
I made a bed amongst winds
and drove the old road
till my heart crashed.

Where's the bypass?

water skips
      undressed
over outcrops

what it says
is

wind
roots in rock

Edge of displaced echoes
air around
and sound
         of bird and plane

A swallow's glittering chitter.

Lying on Long Tongue – sun
diffused in mist – easy sleep,
without waking.

1 June 2003

At this height, two thousand feet above sea level, May blossom arrives late – and then only below the wind line on squat trees in tight cloughs.

It was stotting rain at the end of my shift in the café, but I wanted to take pictures of the hawthorn in bloom and to inhale the scent, so drove down into the South Tyne Valley to the tree where I had taken pictures two years ago when my 'exile' began and where I wrote the *Hawthorn* for the *Ballad of Jamie Allan*.

there is a hawthorn on a hill
there is a hawthorn growing
it set its roots against the wind
the worrying wind that's blowing
its berries are red its blossom so white
I thought that it was snowing...

As I approached the tree, three hares scattered and I saw the lightning-divided trunk as ripped apart – rather than a flailing couple in a cruel but ecstatic dance. Death in dance.

MIDSUMMER

a blood-coloured star
above the swell of a reclining woman
backlit by sun sunk
behind the skunk hills
at midnight

LATE START

and the day
behind blinds
begun

shadows
on a distant hill
a passing car

the phone rings
am I in?

16 August

When I woke this morning I was groggy after working for eight hours in the café's take-away hatch selling drinks, sandwiches, burgers, bacon buns and a range of cakes to a continuous queue of hungry and thirsty bikers, cyclists and cars full of families. The hatch is barely more than a cupboard – a small cramped place in an annex off the kitchen and facing the entrance. Vending from there, meeting demand *en route*, slightly eases the pressure on the women working inside the café.

And work is fast in the kitchen. Cauldrons of hot soup, large pans of steaming water, a vat of bubbling chip fat, one oven baking bread and cakes and another roasting meat. A whirl of pan stirring, dealing out portions, filling orders, peeling, chopping vegetables and fruit, dish washing, ploughing dough, slapping pastry, whisking, whipping eggs, cutting and slicing – all sidestepped by waitresses bringing and collecting orders. Generations work in the café, grannies, mothers, daughters – some from the Alston Moor side of the escarpment and others from villages below tucked in amongst the East Fells and directly in the path of the Helm Wind. These are its children and they can be as fast and furious.

Jackie, who is responsible for keeping my hatch display supplied, shouts above the bustling kitchen:

'Tom, do you need more muffin?'

'Only as much as I can get.'

When it closed I washed dishes and cleaned up, then ate dinner in the empty café at a table next to the French windows. During my meal a thunderstorm travelled over and on to the hills of Dumfries. Now the sky is clear and the air crisp, the sun is low over the Solway Firth, some fifty miles away – and I'm drunk with it.

Sightseers in a lay-by
seek discernible facts
from a dissembling landscape,

like midday sun on the fleece of sheep
that lie and watch them drink
from polystyrene cups
filled from flasks, and photograph.

Banks of cloud stack up and pass.
A low owl blows in, easy
as a breath of thistle.

The moon struck
a set of headlights over the hill
and in my face.

The dead don't remember us.

2 September

a silver-thin sunset dusted gold
obscures the valley
backlit larches on a pencil line of distant hills
the slow mist's opaque drift

My five-year-old grandson, Ottis, is staying here for a couple of weeks. It's been a surprise to find how easy it is to have him around. I was thinking that his complications are not so difficult to resolve as those of his uncles but really they may be more complex. However, the dialogue between us is open and free of boundaries and there is a calm respect for each other, making our separate journeys comfortable, skipping the sometime reserve of overlapping generations. But these thoughts are all new and need time to grow.

A glass of wine and a homesick meadow pipit calls on a fence that fields the fell. When a curlew swallows a whirlpool of song Ottis, calling himself *Samurai-Jack*, leaps from a tabletop flapping his arms, showing how a swan takes off.

I think I'll stay here another year.

BOOGIE-WOOGIE

how seamlessly boogie-woogie
becomes rock and roll

crows and gulls, airborne
in a north-easterly,
pass over the pass

'al reet, then'

her back to the blast
her wool hood up

crows skitter

all those years
keeping a low profile

it wasn't difficult

ANABATIC

at first they recce,
easy

around the edge
of breath

then gathered gangs
unleash
and breach

but the wind has no objectives,
riding the slope of my roof

Worked at home until 2.30 p.m. – it was a struggle between appetite and attainment.

As I walked through the hill mist to Fiends Fell a large bird flipped over the close horizon, just high enough to reveal its underside as it peeled back below the escarpment. So light-coloured beneath and large that I thought *heron*, but moments later a buzzard appeared in silhouette, lifting to eye-level to assess the danger. When I reached the summit the raptor was gone. It had perched just below the oncoming clouds on a reclining limestone boulder patched with buzzard-coloured lichen, which offered draughty shelter from the fast cold Atlantic wind. There was another rock at its base and together they formed a rough chair so I sat and read *The Gypsy Laddie*, and a few other Border Ballads until the cold forced me to close the book.

> *'Tis not Frost that freezes fell*
> *Nor blawin Snaw's Inclemency;*
> *Tis not sic Cauld that makes me numb,*
> *But my Love's Heart grown cauld to me*

The mist lifted and the sky lowered, shrouding the surrounding peaks with dark smoky blues and a band of rosy gold on the distant snow line. I strolled through the heather and whipped grass, stopping occasionally to gaze at the rich green sphagnum mosses. Aware of a sudden calm I began to wonder how long the wind had been silent: did I catch the very instant it stopped, or slowly become conscious of its absence? Then I heard a noise like a thin wind rising through reeds, but nothing stirred except the air some twenty feet above where I saw a fast-moving shadow, a wide massive sweep of starlings. They made no sound save thousands of wings flapping, or *flaffing* as I'd earlier read in *Lord Thomas and Fair Annie*:

There war four an twontie gray goshawks
A flaffin their wings sae wide
To flaff the stour thra off the road
That fair Annie did ride

They swept out into the mist on either side of me like the hurried rustling of a long silk dress echoing in an empty corridor. When I moved on, the winds welled up out of silence as if they'd parted to let the flock through.

Pulling a scarf across my face and my hat down to meet it I followed sheep trails towards a cairn overlooking the Eden Valley, to enjoy the gloaming from there.

As I approached the cairn a large bird silently lifted its dark form and slipped into the rising dusk. For a moment I wondered had I really seen it or was it the same bird, always ahead of me, just out of sight.

an alert kestrel
slung on a gust
preens on a post

am I too old for steep cloughs,
dribbling sykes,
shaking up shags in sphagnum?

a spray whipped
inverted fall
up Ayle Burn head

when a mind seeks
to know itself
the last place it looks
is the body

a pitched raven takes aloft,
cuts low, swept on an uprush

a breath of grass laid low
slicked by quick light

NEW YEAR'S DAY

the blizzards blown out,
snow blowers go below
sun-white Watch Hill

a growking raven groaks,
my first-foot flying past

23 January 2004

Bright constellations and a half moon's light reflected in the café's frosted roof tiles.

A fierce north-easterly lacerates flesh, spins a tango over a small freezing tarn on Fiends Fell, etching scribbles on ice. In an attempt to find a pattern of direction – to record or even paint the wind – I take pictures.

Reeds bent by rime.
Movement in a still frames the invisible.

5 February

Having slept without the radio to lull me out of insomniac thought and because there was no wind, I woke refreshed, with sunlight on the bed and a horn in my hand – conscious of solitude in a way that's new. There was a taste of spring this morning but I'm unable to attribute that to the bright weather or the stiff cock.

   a thirty-mile-an-hour wind
   clouds shift, shiver out the sun
   a slanting sheet of sleet
   driven over the fells from the east

I heard a pair of golden plover – and saw, for the first time at this height, a solitary lapwing passing over and down into the shelter of the Eden Valley, where there are flocks. A storm cock sang in Alston, but in this place, a thousand feet higher, spring comes more cautiously, strung in wind. It brings snipes, curlews, pipits and a shower of lark song.

a gust of sun
and some bird thinks it's spring

the river in flood
in a misaligned season

although we burn in bed
we bicker above the beck

her breath expects
wind and river rip

8 February

The weather here is overseer. Snow turns to rain.
Light withdraws, hill mists drift to lip Long Tongue.
The woven day diminishes.

   sleet storms veil the fells
   thickens into quick snow

   my pen scratches paper
   flames crack

As I worked I followed the light across my desk as though it were an
errant blanket on a cold night.

   rain rush on glass
   a lump of coal shifts in the grate

   fire meters
   the wind's speed

My bronchial father – pale bony face and large brown eyes – tickles the
flame beneath a simmering kettle as my mother walks up the street
and into sight. She's been cleaning houses on the other side of town.
Sparrows flutter in the gutter, a passing vehicle and his wheezing lungs.
Help me take these booties off, she said at the threshold, the kettle
steaming, my feet are killing me.

9 February

night rides up long slopes
mist fills the valley

overlapping greys
patch a hung-over sky

the faint curve of a distant brow

wind-wracked rains
insist on glass

11 February

Walls shudder.
The floor shakes.

A rabid dog on a long leash leaps,
howls, lurches through power lines.

Lashing out, fast and pugnacious,
a punch-drunk heavyweight on speed.

12 February

Late at night, without a coat and the wind still raging, an old woman from the cottage hospital in Alston, banging on the deserted mortuary window, demanding entry – convinced she is home.

Water drapes over worn flattened rocks,
smooth as curtains.

14 February

Four in the afternoon: a swirling sketch on a tarn's surface. Calligraphic fish and fins feathered and winged by wind as the water freezes. Clouds move slowly past as I drift around the pool until the sun blackens and engraved lines delineate.

After looking into frozen water and into thought I turned and fleetingly caught, behind a parting sky, the moon in alignment with the tarn and dripping sun, before clouds obscured again.

night blows up fast
from the valley

dykes dissolve
in thick fog

I follow my feet home

By mid-afternoon I was chasing cage fever, so wrapped myself in several layers of clothing – leaving no flesh exposed to a riving wind – threw on a backpack and headed down Rickers Gill through patches of wet rushes and stubborn heather to the snow line. As I descended the steep slippery banks of Graining Beck, the stream ran fast below the old stone lime kilns. There was sufficient thaw to swell the waters and I could hear the beck's busy echo long before seeing it. When I eased my way down, trying not to brush against clinging thistles, I slipped and instinctively grabbed at the earth to regain my balance and won a palmful of microscopic pricks in my pores. Further upstream I stepped onto a heron's precisely-placed footprint in the snow. The bird had taken the same route so I followed the prints, wondering how long they'd been there. They ended, after a few yards, amongst thin reeds at the quickening rush of the water's edge. The stream twists and turns and loses height suddenly so that many pools form and banks sheer without footing but sometimes, as it momentarily flattens and meanders, there is a choice of banks to walk. I chose the east with its slightly steeper grassy slope instead of the west with a flattened track through slippery shale. This is the choice I make every time, I thought, jumping from rock to rock across the stream and catching sight of the heron's imprint opposite. It too had taken this route. As I followed its tracks I took photographs and spoke occasionally into a small recorder as the light dimmed.

a heron
criss-crosses the lashing syke,
fast, with sudden thaw,

its spiky tread sunk
in unscuffed snow

patient
and hungry as death

no inkling of urgency
in its measured step

close, almost overlapping,
at the water's edge

The day had been mostly cloudy. It was now 3.30 p.m., fifteen minutes from sunset, and a stiff and potentially hazardous climb to safe footing before the night overtook.

As I approached the tight and sudden confluence of three streams, a half moon slightly brightened the dark sky above the narrows. A heron flew past painting air with its primaries, retracing its tracks and mine. With only the lunar half-light to find my footing up the narrow clough I stepped across rocks to higher ground until I reached the ziggurat-like track, winding up from the remains of a deserted barites mine, which was my way out of there. A low jet roared overhead, rehearsing a raid on Iraq.

> *May the sacred river Ulay mourn you,*
> *along whose banks we walked in our vigour!*
> *May the poor Euphrates mourn you,*
> *whose water we poured in libation from skins!*
>
> *May the young men of Uruk-the-Sheepfold mourn you,*
> *who saw us slay the Bull of Heaven!*
> *May the ploughman mourn you in his furrows*
> *when he sows your name in song* *

When I climbed up to the edge of the fell I took a step into myself and found a predatory instinct. A sneaping wind was blowing around the top of the 'ziggurat' and to stay out of its icy bite for as long as possible I descended again into the deep shadows of the narrow clough to a sheep track level with the stream which would provide shelter up the steep, wind-ripped hill to the damp patch of its source where I would become exposed for the final mile home to the unfettered, unhindered and unhinged gale.

* *Gilgamesh*, trans. Andrew George.

~

AFTER A ROW

A lapwing somersaults spring,
flips over winter and back.

After a fast walk – my limbs
the engine of thought – up long hills
where burn bubbles into beck and clough to gill

beneath a sandstone cliff
balanced on a bed of shale
and held from hurtling by Scots pine
that brush a scrubby sky
with cloud snow scutters,

I found a place to sit
by snapping watta smacking rocks,

and wondered – how would it be for you?

and so, alone, un-alone even,
in my anger, bring you here.

BY WAY OF SAYING

something about nocturnes
about wind about skin

asleep in a pile of pillows
I bring her coffee

to the foot of the bed,
to watch her wake

how does the day take you?
and all of it ahead of us

today becomes her
a perfect fit
bespoke
before she speaks

WORK

As I knelt at a cold stove

waiting for a long draw
to catch my light

and take my time,
my icy element,

a threshing rain
laid into the roof.

When the stove lit
I thought of her
and desire,

and what an exquisite word
that is.

DREAM

I dreamt I wrote a poem,
the day Neil Armstrong died
playing on the radio,

about an afternoon with you in August
so easy and unaccomplished
I forgot it when I woke

and made no effort to recall
until the kettle boiled,
and I remembered

how complex easy is

HOMAGE

a stripper strokes the
slope of her hip; Hokusai
painting mount Fuji

MISS SYNCOPATION

so, she said,
stripped
and slipping into bed,
do you have a copy
of machiavelli's
the prince,
then?

but what she craved
was hard rock
ready to roll

he flopped a soft lob

she pounced – a cat
at a carpet scratch

and blew him to insomnia
by faithless

how would it be
with the goldberg variations?
the late quartets?
bartok? bebop? byrd?
the byrds?

scriabin's whole
exploding atonal hole? john

cage?

TO GOAD MY FRIGGIN PEERS

Fuck the sonnet, I piss upon it
and those who seek to launch
a sinking reputation on it –
as though it were a talismanic indenture,
an entrée to a toothless craft.

Tak those billiards oot ya pocket,
to reach the moon yi need a rocket.

OBJET TROUVE

Don't get me wrong, neighbour,
I'm not ripping the piss,
I just want your dog to stop
shitting on my step.

I may be dissing it,
it could be your bitch.

I'm not saying it is,
I just want her, it, to stop
dropping the poop
on my stoop.

WONGAWONGALAND

doctor Gobbles with his jowly wobbles
wants to stop the sick and jobless
quaffing from his gissy goblets
and break their backs
on the rock of his salvation

he serves a cold buffet of hot wars
to pump the economy for further plunder
and squanders young lives
like bankers on a company junket

if the hungry were hung he'd hang the anger out
incentivise to fuck off and die
or just have a jousting match
of polite poetries

once they bled themselves for a cure
now they only bleed the poor

WHINING WHILE DINING OOT

Ama propa Geordie, me.
aa write propa poetry.
Nobody reads is
and it fuckin grieves is –
but ama propa Geordie, me.

Aa git funding off the Council
for blowin oot me tonsils,
ama propa Geordie, me.
Aa gan ti matches when aa can
an wetch the team gan doon the pan.
Ama propa Geordie, man.

Aa write propa stuff
not like them posh puffs –
that southern tart
that come up here to write aboot
her scented farts.
Ama propa Geordie, me.
Smell the authenticity!

Aa served some time in Durham
(University). Got a discharge with a PhD
aboot a propa Geordie, me.
Not that clumpin slug from Hull
who gets prized for being dull
aa get slavvad oot me skull,
cos ama propa Geordie, me.

If am just a smidgen posh
you know it helps is get the dosh,
aa stash it in the pigeon loft,
burrad never use a word like gosh

when I write me jangling tosh
cos ama propa Geordie, me.

Aa hoyed up with the Common folk,
but still they think that ama joke.
Aa wish that I could get a poke
ama propa Geordie, me.

SQUIRE

hoy me a black suit
sling me a coat
rip up the black shirt
and sling me the red
hang me my black tie
alan hull is dead

roll back the black hills
hoy back the sea
rip up the black flags
and run up the red
hang me my black tie
alan hull is dead

slam down the phone
slam shut the door
open the olives
and break the black bread
lay out the basil
alan hull is dead

THE SHORT-EARED OWL
AS GROUND-NESTING METAPHOR

Roy Fisher said
owl is low
spelt inside out.

L flaps to the front
and the W,
hatched
and flown back,
splays
like a tail
over O
rolled
and nestled

waiting
to
toowoo
again

FOR BOB

The whole sweep
of the day.

If I were Creeley
I'd know what I meant
and make it a poem.
But I'm not
and I don't
and I have.

ESTUARY ENTRIES

That curlew standing
on sea-wracked rock
owns it,
till the tide turns.

*

A collie, off the leash,
in suck-me-in sand,
rounds up the waves.

*

Waders wait
to lead the tide in,
eat the tide out.

*

Following footprints in damp sand
as though my own – already ahead
and behind.

*

Far out onto the estuary
the tide turns under my feet,
runs up ripples of sand,
wraps around my ankles.

*

A flock of gulls
in a confetti flurry
flung along the flood line.

AT THE ESTUARY

sanderlings dig bait,
tailgate the first ripple
of a returning tide

a mercury whisper
of tipped-in light
rushed in, in front of itself

scrow clouds
scuffed aheight

swirls of wrung-out rags

wind riven
wind driven waves
belly flop on rock

what the heart loves
loves not the heart

WINTER MIGRANTS

a mass of moth-eaten cloud
threadbare and spun across
a bullish moon

an animal wakes
when I walk in winter,

wrapped against
a withering wind,

solitary,

on a Solway flat

winter migrants gather
in long black lines

along a silver sleek

heads held back,
throats
        thrust toward
an onshore rush

occasionally cruciform,
        static
in a flying wind

as though
in obeisance
        to the sea

each tide a season
in the pecking mall

retracing steps
    washed out
by whimpering silt

they call as I approach,
    an upright spelk
on their shelf,

     gathering my notes
and theirs

we scavenge
    ahead of our shadows

waiting for what

the tide brings in
or leaves out

purple,
  hedged cloud
edged gold

 hung
on silver slates
  of sand

diverted
  leaps of light
surrender water

risen
  from rivulets
roughed
  from rage

repealing waves
  repeat

a curlew's
  estuary echo

who,
  but you
 and the wind's
wake?

ACKNOWLEDGEMENTS

Thanks to the editors of *The Nation*, *Chicago Review*, *Poetry Chicago*, *London Review of Books*, the *Recluse*, *Edinburgh Review*, *Woodland Pattern Book Center*, *3:AM Magazine*, *Friday Night Boys*, and *Berfrois*.